GDPR Handbook for small businesses

Be ready in 21 days (or less)

Olivier Staquet

Copyright © 2018 Olivier Staquet

All rights reserved.

ISBN: 1981826394
ISBN-13: 978-1981826391

DISCLAIMER

The thoughts and ideas listed in this book are aimed to help the reader with a perspective on GDPR implementation and assist through defining steps to build or challenge his/her compliance roadmap. The thoughts or ideas are not legal opinions and shall have no legal liability whatsoever.

Further, the opinions, thoughts, and ideas mentioned in this book are the personal opinions of the author as an individual and do not have any correlation with any company or organization for which the author has worked or is working.

CONTENTS

1	Introduction	1
2	Learn the basics	6
3	Practical Action Plan for Data Controllers	10
4	Practical Action Plan for Data Processors	16
5	Take Organizational Measures	19
6	The Checklist	23
7	Additional Considerations	26
8	How to Use the Templates?	34
9	Sources	46

1 INTRODUCTION

What is the General Data Protection Regulation?

The General Data Protection Regulation (GDPR) is being brought in to strengthen and unify data protection of all individuals within the European Union (EU). The regulation was adopted on April 27, 2016 and will be enforced from May 25, 2018. As it is a regulation (not a directive), the national governments do not have to pass local laws for the legislation to become effective.

GDPR deals with the protection of personal data, which includes common elements such as name, gender, address, email address and phone number but also includes anything that could "reasonably" identify an individual, such as IP address, car license plate, bank account or MAC address. In addition, specific measures will be introduced for the processing of sensitive personal data (e.g. healthcare, religion and political allegiance).

The data is the responsibility of the data's owner (as before) but the third-party providers are also directly accountable. Both must take appropriate measures to protect individuals' personal data and to show compliance. This need to demonstrate compliance is based on four key elements:
1. set up internal policies;
2. keep records of all processing activities;
3. regularly review and evaluate data protection measures;
4. and adopt/approve established codes of conduct.

For a serious infringement of GDPR rules (such as violating privacy laws or not having the required consent to process the data), companies can be fined up to €20 million or 4% of their annual turnover. In general, the EU will take a tiered approach to fines depending on the severity of the infringements.

This will strengthen individuals' rights, enabling them to access, correct, delete and lock data concerning themselves. Depending on the legal basis of the processing activity, GDPR also includes the right to be forgotten (relating to policies regarding the retention of data) and the right to data portability (enables a customer to download a "package" of their own data, to own it or to transfer it to another provider).

The regulation also includes the obligation to notify authorities and customers if there is a data breach. In the case of data hacking or theft, the authorities and customers must be notified within 72 hours. A data breach is not only about data theft but also about accidental deletion of data.

The last important core concept of the regulation is the idea of privacy by design and by default. Privacy by design means that the data protection aspects are directly integrated into the early development of business processes for products and services. Privacy by default means that the privacy settings must be set at a high level by default.

It is important to note that the purpose of the regulation is to protect the rights of the individuals and not to stop all business initiatives.

All the concepts about data privacy in GDPR are not new. The majority of these ideas and requirements already exist in various forms in the different EU member countries.

To remember in a simple way…

Do what you do with less data, more accountability and more sanctions. Privacy is now citizen-centric and recognized as a fundamental right.

Why This Handbook?

The new regulation on data privacy in the EU is a big book written by lawyers, academics, politicians and lobbyists to finally enforce better protection of individuals' privacy. The decision to pass a regulation instead of a directive is a positive move for citizens of the EU. If you are not familiar with the difference, here is a (hopefully) simple explanation: A directive is "strong advice/a guideline" suggested by the EU that must be transposed at some point in the local laws of the member countries. A regulation is a law defined by the EU that is enforced immediately for all member countries.

GDPR is a regulation (i.e. a law) defined by the EU. In a nutshell, the objective of this regulation is to protect the privacy of EU citizens. The regulation is applied worldwide insofar as it concerns European citizens wherever they are or companies with a subsidiary in the EU.

Unfortunately, this regulation of 88 pages and 99 articles is not easy reading. It is complex to translate into an action plan for a small company or a small non-profit organization.

Large corporations already have a risk and compliance department or a legal department to take charge of this and adapt the company's existing processes to meet the requirements of GDPR. In these companies, all the processes are currently being listed, documented and adapted, if required. But the regulation also affects small and medium-sized businesses (SMBs) and non-profit organization (NPOs), in other words every company that has employees or customers. Most of these organizations do not have an army of lawyers to read the regulation, convert it into an action plan and get ready for enforcement on May 25, 2018.

The purpose of this handbook is therefore to describe an easy-to-use action plan to help SMBs and NPOs get ready for GDPR. It was written by the Managing Director of an SMB while he addressed compliance requirements for his company. During the writing of this handbook, the recommendations and guidelines evolved; the author updated the handbook as much as possible on the basis of currently available information. It is not a legal study of the regulation, so there are no exact references to the regulation or the articles within.

If you have ideas, templates, additional information that can help other readers, feel free to contact the author via the website: https://www.gdpr-handbook.eu/.

Who Is This Handbook For?

GDPR applies to anyone who provides goods or services to people in the EU or monitors their behavior; this also applies to companies outside the EU but that provide goods or services to EU citizens, either within the EU or further afield.

GDPR covers your activities that involve the collection, storage or processing of an EU citizen's personal data. When talking about data protection, most people think about customers and marketing operations like newsletters or sales prospects. The scope is much broader and covers all activities related to employees and daily operations, in brief, all activities related to your business.

With such a broad scope, one of the key activities is to identify all processes and activities in your company that include the processing of personal data of individuals of all types: customers, prospects, employees, partners, volunteers, etc. With this in mind, you will be able to take appropriate measures.

The protection of individuals' data is your responsibility as an organization. Any breach of GDPR will cost your business a lot in terms of money and image.

To remember in a simple way…

This handbook is for all small businesses and small NPOs that process personal data. By process, we mean collecting, storing, archiving and using. By personal data, we mean all personal information about customers, employees, volunteers, etc.

How to Use This Handbook?

This handbook is divided into five major sections each representing a step toward compliance.

The first step is called "Learn the Basics." During this step, you will first be familiarized with some basic definitions related to data protection. In the definitions, you will find the notions of Data Controller and Data Processor; these are required to complete step one and identify if you are a Data Controller and/or a Data Processor. The regulation differs depending on which category you belong to.

The second and third steps cover the action plans for the Data Controller and Data Processor respectively. The action plan for the Data Controller (who determines the purpose and the means of the processing activities) is a bit longer due to the regulation's requirements. The action plans described in this handbook cover the requirements to be ready in a practical way for the introduction of GDPR and by applying our advice, you can be confident you will be ready.

To fulfill your requirements, there are two additional steps. The fourth step is how to take organizational measures to ensure you are ready. The last step is the data protection checklist, the purpose of which is to highlight some data protection topics that you should consider within your organization.

The additional considerations cover some important principles linked to GDPR. These additional considerations give some ideas for implementing the data protection processes in your organization and some answers to the questions you might have about specific topics, for example international transfer, legal basis for processing or data portability.

The last chapter gives you recommendations on how to use the templates (in various formats like Excel or Word) available on the website: https://www.gdpr-handbook.eu/. These templates are useful tools to help your organization meet the regulation's requirements.

To conclude this introduction, we strongly suggest you keep an eye on the advice given by the Article 29 Working Party (WP29) (more info on http://ec.europa.eu/justice/data-protection/index_en.htm) and follow the advice and recommendations of the local authority for data protection active in your country (see http://ec.europa.eu/justice/data-protection/bodies/authorities/index_en.htm).

2 LEARN THE BASICS

GDPR is essential to protecting the privacy and personal data of EU citizens. It comes in the form of a thick legal document with specific vocabulary that is not so obvious for non-legal people.

The first step is to become more familiar with the terms used in GDPR and understand whether you are on the Data Controller side or the Data Processor side.

Let's start with the definitions.

Definitions

By reading the regulation and during the GDPR journey, you may encounter specific vocabulary that is not so obvious if you are not a lawyer. Below, you will find specific definitions, with the most important part in bold.

Anonymous Data: Data which is **neither personal nor pseudonymous**.

Article 29 Working Party (WP29) or Group 29: Working group made up of a representative from the data protection authority of each EU member country, the European Data Protection Supervisor and the European Commission to **provide guidelines and recommendations** to the public on matters relating to data protection.

Data Breach: A data breach is a security incident in which **personal**

data is copied, transmitted, viewed, stolen or used by an unauthorized individual. **Accidental deletion** of personal data is also considered a data breach.

Data Controller: The natural or legal person, public authority, agency or any other entity that alone or jointly with others **determines the purpose and means of processing personal data**.

Data Portability: Right for the Data Subject to **receive the personal data**, which they have provided to a Data Controller, in a structured, commonly used and **machine-readable format**, and **to transmit the data to another Data Controller**.

Data Processor: A natural or legal person, public authority, agency or any other entity that **processes personal data on behalf of the Data Controller**.

Data Recipient: A natural or legal person, public authority, agency or any other entity **to whom data is disclosed** whether a third party or not. However, authorities that may receive data in the framework of an inquiry shall not be regarded as recipients.

Data Retention: **Policies relating to persistent data and records management** for meeting legal and business data archive requirements.

Data Subject: **A living individual to whom personal data relates**.

Lawful Processing or Legal Basis for Processing: **Legal basis defining why a Data Controller can process personal data** (also referred to as "conditions for processing"). The lawful processing conditions are explained in Chapter 7.

National Supervisory Authority: **Official organization** active in a country that **oversees the privacy protection** of individuals. The list of these authorities is available on http://ec.europa.eu/justice/data-protection/bodies/authorities/index_en.htm.

Personal Data: Any information relating to an **identified or identifiable natural person** who can be identified, **directly or indirectly, by reference to an identifier** such as a name, an identification number, location data, unique identifier or to one or more factors specific to the physical, physiological, genetic, mental, economic, cultural, social or gender identity of that person.

Processing Activity: **Any operation or set of operations that are performed on personal data**, whether by automatic means, such as collection, recording, organization, storage, adaptation, alteration, retrieval, consultation, use, disclosure by transmission, dissemination, making available, alignment, combination, blocking, deletion or destruction.

Pseudonymization: Procedure by which the **most identifying fields** within a data record are **replaced by one or more artificial identifiers**, or pseudonyms.

Pseudonyms: Personal data that **cannot be attributed to a specific Data Subject without the use of additional information**, if such additional information is kept separate and subject to technical and organizational measures to ensure non-attribution.

Sensitive Personal Data: Personal data relating to **race or ethnic** origin, **political** opinions, **religion** or **philosophical** beliefs, **sexual orientation or gender identity**, **trade union** membership and activities, **genetic or biometric** data, **health or sex life, administrative sanctions, judgments, criminal or suspected offenses, convictions**, or related security measures.

Third Party: Any natural or legal person, public authority, agency or any **other entity other than the Data Subject, the Data Controller, the Data Processor and the persons who**, under the direct authority of the Data Controller or Data Processor, **are authorized to process the data**.

Who Are You?

The first question is to determine if you are a Data Controller, a Data Processor or both. Though that sentence uses the term "you," the reality is that your organization is actually the Data Controller, the Data Processor or both. It is a question of what role your organization plays, both internally and in relation to external organizations. Within your organization, you might then choose specific people to fulfil the GDPR requirements for these roles, so "you" and "the organization" are used interchangeably when discussing this element.

The Data Controller defines the purpose and means of the processing of personal data. Basically, if you are processing the personal data of your employees, your customers or the members of your organization, you are a Data Controller and you must be compliant with the set of rules defined in step 2.

The Data Processor processes personal data on behalf of the Data Controller. It means that if you are a software provider and your organization processes the personal data for another organization, you are a Data Processor.

When you are a Data Processor, you are most likely also a Data Controller. For example, as a Data Processor, you might provide software to other organizations and your role is limited to data processing for those specific activities, but to provide your service, you have employees and, for this part, you are the Data Controller. In the same mindset, if you are creating or processing some personal data to build up a new database, you become a Data Controller for this additional part.

To summarize, all organizations are Data Controllers but not all organizations are Data Processors. If you process data for another organization (e.g. software as a service), you are also a Data Processor. All your activities as Data Controller and Data Processor should be clearly separated and documented.

3 PRACTICAL ACTION PLAN FOR DATA CONTROLLERS

You are now familiar with the terms and—yes, you understood well—all organizations fall under the remit of Data Controller. If you process your customers' or employees' data in an electronic way, you are a Data Controller and you must consider the action plan in this chapter.

Let's now get ready for GDPR in a practical way.

Assign a Data Protection Officer if Applicable

The Data Protection Officer (DPO) is the contact person for the authorities. S/he is responsible for keeping the Registry of Data Processing Activities, for notifying the authorities in case of data breaches and for defining internal processes in case of questions regarding personal data. The DPO should be independent from the board of directors to avoid a conflict of interest and to guarantee impartiality. S/he has a central role in data protection and must be actively involved in all issues related to the protection of personal data, in a timely manner.

To remain pragmatic and depending on your organization, assign a DPO only if required.

Based on the official regulation text, a DPO is mandatory for businesses where core activities require regular and systematic monitoring of Data Subjects on a large scale and where core activities consist of processing sensitive data on a large scale.

This requirement is not so obvious and you are perhaps wondering what is meant by regular, systematic and large scale. You should use your common sense here due to the lack of an official threshold. The number of entries in your database does not really matter: a hundred or a million entries does not make a huge difference. The key approach is to judge your processing activities with a critical eye. If the public could see it as a threat to their privacy, it is better to assign a DPO. If not, you can live without one.

Keep the Inventory

The inventory is the most important part of GDPR. It takes the form of the Registry of Data Processing Activities (hereafter also just called the registry) and is strongly recommended for all companies. This document is very important and must be kept updated at all times. It is the starting point for GDPR compliance.

From a regulation perspective, the registry is not mandatory for organizations employing fewer than 250 employees unless:
- the processing is likely to result in a risk to the rights and freedoms of Data Subjects or
- the processing is not occasional or
- the processing includes sensitive personal data.

In practical terms, as soon as the National Supervisory Authority receives a complaint from a Data Subject, your organization must demonstrate compliance with GDPR (e.g. data minimization, legal basis for processing and ensuring security measures are in place). This is why the registry is strongly recommended as it will be relatively quick and straightforward for you to collate and submit the information required by the authority.

At a glance, this registry could be seen as a pure regulatory document, not interesting or complex to set up. In fact, this registry is the cornerstone of your data protection strategy. Basically, it will contain all processing activities that your company performs on personal data. For each activity, you will have to check, investigate, document and note how you will obtain the Data Subjects' consent. In the end, this will give you a clear view of all your personal data processing activities. Thanks to this analysis, you will be able to pinpoint where you must adapt your activities to be in line with the regulation, when you must ask for the Data Subjects' consent and also put a stop to any illegal activities. In brief, this document will be a constant work in progress.

The register must be held internally in the company. As soon as the authorities receive a complaint, this will be the first document they will ask you to provide and you will have to prove that your actual processes match the description you provided.

The best way to start is to use the spreadsheet enclosed in this handbook's toolbox. The guidelines for using the template are explained in Chapter 8.

To conclude, remember that the registry is a living animal. Each time you develop or create a new activity that involves personal data, do not forget to update your registry. This will ensure that you have checked the important aspects like consent, retention policy and the security measures for this activity.

Dig Deeper for High-risk Activities

GDPR includes some obligations for high-risk activities and for the processing of sensitive personal data. For these activities, you must conduct a Data Protection Impact Assessment (DPIA). A DPIA is a process to identify and reduce the privacy risks of new projects or new practices. It is an integral part of the concept of privacy by design introduced with GDPR.

The objective of the DPIA is to minimize the risks for the Data Subjects, preventing illegal processing and implementing privacy by design and by default. After applying the measures to minimize the risks, some residual risks may remain. If the residual risk is still too high, you should consult the authorities. It is important to note that you must conduct the assessment before starting the activity.

The DPIA is the responsibility of the Data Controller only. This assessment is a gatekeeper for when a type of processing is likely to result in a high risk to the rights and freedoms of natural persons. The Data Processor (third-party processor) must assist the Data Controller in this process. The DPO must also be involved in the DPIA, but only in an advisory role. S/he must control its execution but cannot be the one to complete it.

When to Conduct a Data Protection Impact Assessment?

You must conduct the DPIA before starting the activity. A single assessment may suffice. Later, when the risk evolves, it will require review. The DPIA is particularly required in the three cases below:

- Systematic and extensive evaluation based on automated processing, including profiling, and on which decisions with legal or similar effects are based.
- Processing on a large scale of sensitive data or personal data relating to criminal convictions and offenses.
- Systematic monitoring of a publicly accessible area on a large scale.

The scope of these cases could be seen as quite vague, which is why the Privacy Commission of Belgium created a list to illustrate when a DPIA is mandatory. Though this list was written by a Belgium authority, it should be useful regardless of where your organization is based or doing business within the EU. This list can serve as a basis for you to evaluate if you must conduct a DPIA:

- Use of biometric data to identify individuals.
- Use of genetic data.
- When personal data is collected through a third party to make a decision to authorize/deny/stop a service.
- When the purpose of the activity is to evaluate the financial solvency of the individual or to generate a risk profile.
- When the personal data collected can jeopardize the physical health of an individual in case of data breaches.
- Financial or sensitive data used for another purpose than the initial purpose for which it has been collected.
- The communication or making available to the public of personal data concerning many individuals.
- Use of personal data to evaluate and predict professional services, economic situation, health, preferences, personal interests, reliability, behavior, localization or trips of the Data Subject.
- When the profiling of physical persons is done on a large scale.
- Large-scale processing of personal data of vulnerable physical persons (e.g. children) for another purpose than the initial purpose for which the data has been collected.
- When multiple Data Controllers would like to create an application or system to process data for a sector or professional segment, and for which sensitive data is used.
- When the process is to store the knowledge, performance, skills or state of mental health of students.

For all of the above cases, a DPIA is strongly recommended.

How to Conduct a Data Protection Impact Assessment?

A DPIA is a document that covers the analysis of risk from the Data Subject's point of view. As it is conducted before starting the project, all potential threats to the privacy of the individuals are described and analyzed. This first analysis results in a good overview of the absolute risk.

The document also covers all measures taken to minimize the absolute risk identified with the processing activity. These measures can be technical or organizational. After applying them, only the residual risk remains. It must be explained and covered in the DPIA.

It is a good approach to involve Data Subjects in this analysis to obtain and document their opinions about the process and the residual risk. At the end of the assessment, if the residual risk is still high, you must consult your National Supervisory Authority.

Data Breach Response Plan

GDPR introduces for the first time a general data breach notification at EU level, requiring both notification to the National Supervisory Authority and to the Data Subjects affected by the breach.

When a data breach is detected, the Data Controller must notify the National Supervisory Authority within 72 hours. This notification must be done when the individual is likely to suffer from some form of damage, for example identity theft or breach of confidentiality.

If the data breach could potentially put individuals at risk, the Data Controller must notify the Data Subjects without delay. There is an important exception here: notification to the Data Subjects is not required when the data breach is not likely to cause any risk to their rights and freedom.

It means that if the Data Controller implemented appropriate technical and organizational protection measures, and if those measures were applied to the personal data affected by the data breach (e.g. encryption), the Data Subjects do not need to be notified because the data is unusable.

The notification of the data breach is an important topic for the authorities, which is why you should set up a data breach response plan in your organization.

This process should be clearly defined for all employees and members of your organization. They should know that in case of data breach, they must notify the DPO (if you have one), or the Managing Director or the relevant contact in your organization. This person will fill out the notification template (enclosed in this handbook) with all the required information.

This template serves as a communication medium between you, the authorities and the Data Subjects (depending on the impact). It means that the notification should be structured clearly, and written in a clear and comprehensive way.

4 PRACTICAL ACTION PLAN FOR DATA PROCESSORS

You have now fulfilled all your obligations as a Data Controller. This chapter is dedicated to the Data Processor. The regulation is less constraining for Data Processors because they process the data on behalf of the Data Controller. It is the latter who defines the purpose and the means of the processing. As a Data Processor, it is important to note that it is your responsibility to assist the Data Controller and to warn them when they cross the line of legality.

If you are also a Data Processor, let's continue to get ready in a practical way.

Keep the Inventory

As said before, the inventory is critical for the Data Controller. It takes the form of the Registry of Data Processing Activities (hereafter more commonly referred to as the registry), in which the Data Controller checks and documents all personal data activities.

The Data Processor is also obliged to maintain such a registry, but with fewer details. This registry consists of the identity of the Data Controllers, the categories of personal data, and the technical and organizational security measures in place to protect the personal data provided by the Data Controllers.

As a Data Processor, you must keep this registry up to date because of your involvement in the data processing. The registry allows you to identify the sensitivity level of the personal data that you are processing and to check the security measures in place to protect that data.

From a regulation perspective and as said before, the registry is not mandatory for organizations employing fewer than 250 employees unless:
- the processing is likely to result in a risk to the rights and freedoms of Data Subjects or
- the processing is not occasional or
- the processing includes sensitive personal data.

As you are a Data Processor, you are likely to provide processing activities for Data Controllers who must have a registry. If this is the case, it is advisable for the Data Processor to have a registry too. Additionally, we suggest using the regulation to your competitive advantage: the Data Controllers (your customers) will want more safeguards regarding their processing activities and your demonstration of compliance with GDPR will reassure them.

To simplify the creation of your registry, you can use the spreadsheet included in this handbook's toolbox. Chapter 8 contains guidelines on how to use the template properly.

To conclude, we will repeat what we said about the Data Controller's inventory: Remember that it is a living animal. It is your responsibility to keep it up to date, to check regularly that the data is still secured properly and that the Data Controller's information is still valid.

Data Breach Response Plan

When a data breach is detected, the Data Processor must notify the affected Data Controller as soon as possible because the latter should activate a specific action plan in the scope of GDPR. This notification is required when the individual is likely to suffer from some form of damage, such as identity theft or breach of confidentiality.

Notification of the data breach is important for the authorities and failure to do so could lead to heavy sanctions for the Data Controller. As the Data Processor, it is your responsibility to support the Data Controller, which is why you should set up a data breach response plan in your organization.

This process should be clearly defined for all employees and members of your organization. If a data breach occurs, the person who first notices the breach must notify the DPO (if you have one), the Managing Director or a relevant point of contact. This person will fill out the notification template with all the necessary information.

There are no specific requirements for the communication to the Data Controller but you can use the same template for a data breach notification as that used by the Data Controller to notify the authorities (enclosed in this handbook).

5 TAKE ORGANIZATIONAL MEASURES

So far, only guidelines required from a purely regulatory perspective have been addressed. However, to make sure that everything goes smoothly within your organization, it is good practice to take some organizational measures. For this, the regulation introduces the concepts of privacy by design and privacy by default.

Privacy by design means that all products, services and processes must protect users' privacy. Privacy by default means that, by default, all parameters should be set at a high level of privacy and the Data Processor should only ask for the minimum information required for the processing activity.

To manage that, you should ensure all members of the organization are aware of GDPR. You should educate your employees and partners about the regulation and its requirements. This is one of the most important organizational measures.

Additionally, you should put some internal processes in place to be ready to handle common requests like Data Subjects wanting access to their data.

Education and Awareness

Data protection awareness does not happen overnight in an organization; rather, it is an ongoing, long-term project. You should communicate clearly to your employees about the nature of the regulation, how it will affect their daily job and why it is important.

Explaining all the legal details of the regulation is inefficient and not necessarily helpful. GDPR should be explained in simple terms, and more specifically in actionable terms. You should concentrate your communication efforts on the concrete actions that your staff should take to protect personal data and avoid any data breaches.

It might be suitable for you to present GDPR and the impact on your business to all your employees in a single slide deck. It is important to show that data protection is critical at every single level of the company. It is also advisable to keep track of the attendees in case of inspection by the authorities.

This kind of presentation will allow your employees to raise questions. As a bonus, you will probably get additional insights into processes that you are not aware of. For example, an assistant might be using customers' email addresses to send them Christmas cards and storing all related data on Mailchimp. This is not a problem, but you should be aware of it to complete your registry and check the privacy terms of Mailchimp.

As for IT security, an awareness program should be set up that is mandatory for everyone. Ideally, employees should partake annually to be sure they are up to date, perhaps using a memorable date for this meeting, for example Data Privacy Day on January 28 (assuming it is on a business day). Again, we recommend keeping track of the attendees to show to the authorities your willingness to be compliant.

In addition to the internal awareness program, do not hesitate to share the information with your business partners and vendors. Tell them that you care about data protection, you aim to be ready for the introduction of GDPR and that you expect them to do so as well. It is also your responsibility to ensure that your suppliers and partners meet the GDPR requirements. It is not necessary to audit them, but you have to at least cover your organization in the terms of the contract.

It is also advisable to update the terms of employment, codes of conduct or other similar documents to add details regarding data protection. The objective is to inform employees that any breach or misuse of data will lead to disciplinary measures. This is also useful for keeping track of employees' acceptance of these updates, to show to the authorities that you are taking data protection seriously.

Dealing with Data Subject Access Requests

As stated before, one of the most important rights for the individuals is the right of access. This is one of the key aspects to be enforced by GDPR. This right of access means that you should supply to the individual the personal data that you store on this specific individual, if the request is valid. Note that this right of access has existed for a long time in most national laws across the EU. It is not a new aspect of the regulation and it is good to set up a process for when this kind of request arrives.

When you receive an access request, you must supply the information to the individual within 40 calendar days upon receipt of the request. You should provide the information in a form that is clear for a layperson, with all codification explained. And, above all, you must ensure that you give the personal information only to the individual concerned. For instance, you should not normally provide such information over the phone as you cannot confirm the identity of the requester.

The following steps will help you manage these requests:

1. Appoint a coordinator responsible for the response to the access request and give them visibility across the organization. It is important to inform your staff about the necessity of the coordinator and their functions and responsibilities.

2. All Data Subject access matters should be submitted to the coordinator.

3. Check the validity of the access request. Ensure that it is in writing.

4. Check that sufficient material has been supplied to formally identify the individual. Within your organization, you should define criteria to be assessed to identify an individual. This may be the signature, an ID number in combination with the name and address, or date of birth. It should not be possible for a third party to provide the material to lodge a false access request.

5. Check that sufficient information has been supplied to locate the data. If it is unclear what kind of data is being requested, you should ask the Data Subject for more information. This could involve identifying the databases, locations or files to be searched. You may also ask the Data Subject to provide a description of the interactions they have had with the organization.

6. Log the receipt date for each valid request.

7. Keep a note of all steps taken to locate and collect data: if different divisions of the organization are involved, have the steps signed off by the appropriate people.

8. Monitor the response process and observe the time limit of 40 calendar days.

9. Supply the data in an intelligible form (include an explanation of terms if necessary). Also provide a description of purpose, disclosure and sources of data (unless contrary to public interest). Tag the supplied documents with references (this can be a simple number). Have the response signed off by an appropriate person.

6 THE CHECKLIST

This is the last step on your GDPR readiness journey. This book has so far covered the regulation's topics to get ready in a practical way and will now conclude with the checklist. If you can tick "Yes" to all the questions in it, congratulations, because it means that your organization is ready for GDPR. Above all, it also means that you are actively taking care of individuals' rights and data privacy. The checklist covers some aspects of the regulation but also data protection in general.

Let's go through it to identify any gaps in your organization and identify the appropriate measures to take.

Checklist on Data Protection Policy

A. Fairly obtaining data

A.1. When we collected information about individuals, were they made aware of the intended use of that information?

A.2. Are people made aware of any disclosures of their data to third parties?

A.3. Have we obtained people's consent for any secondary use of their personal data? Which use might not be obvious to them?

A.4. Can we describe our data collection practices as open, transparent and upfront?

B. Purpose specification

B.1. Are we clear about the purpose (or purposes) for which we keep personal information?

B.2. Is this purpose clear for the individuals that are in your database?

B.3. Has anyone been assigned to maintaining a list of all data sets and their purposes?

C. Use and disclosure of information

C.1. Are there defined rules for usage or disclosure of information?

C.2. Are staff members aware of these rules?

C.3. Are the individuals aware of the usage or disclosure of their personal data? Would they be surprised if they learned about them? (Consider whether individuals' consent should be obtained for these uses and disclosure.)

D. Security

D.1. Is there a list of security measures in place for each data set?

D.2. Is someone responsible for the development and review of these measures?

D.3. Are these measures appropriate to the sensitivity of the personal data we keep?

D.4. Are our computers and databases password-protected, and encrypted if appropriate?

D.5. Are our computers, servers and files securely locked away from unauthorized people?

E. Being adequate, relevant and not excessive

E.1. Do we collect all the information we need to serve our purpose(s) effectively, and to deal with individuals in a fair and comprehensive manner?

E.2. Have we checked to make sure that all the information we collect is relevant, and not excessive, for our specified purpose(s)?

E.3. If an individual asked us to justify every piece of information we hold about them, could we do so? Does a policy exist for this?

F. Accuracy and updates

F.1. Do we check our data for accuracy?

F.2. Do we know how time-sensitive the personal data stored in our database is, i.e. how likely is it to become inaccurate over time if not updated?

F.3. Do we take measures to keep our databases up to date?

G. Retention time

G.1. Is there a clear statement on how long information is to be retained?

G.2. Are we clear on the legal requirements that apply to us on data retention?

G.3. Do we regularly purge the data we no longer need from our databases, for example data related to former customers or staff members?

G.4. Do we have a policy on personal data deletion upon completion of the purpose for which we obtained the data?

H. Right of access

H.1. Is anyone responsible for handling access requests?

H.2. Are there clear procedures in place for dealing with such requests?

H.3. Do these procedures guarantee compliance with GDPR and national requirements?

7 ADDITIONAL CONSIDERATIONS

This chapter is to be used as an addendum to the action plan. The objective is to cover specific aspects and terminology of the regulation and to give some tips for handling specific cases.

First, the chapter covers the legal basis for processing possibilities mentioned in the regulation. This is the foundation on which a Data Controller can process personal data. It is a very important topic in your privacy strategy because the selection of the legal basis comes with critical consequences that will affect the activities required for compliance with GDPR.

The chapter also looks at questions of data portability and international transfer, as well as providing some tips to handle these questions in a pragmatic way.

Legal Basis for Processing

For the processing of personal data to be legal under GDPR, you need first to identify a legal basis. This is also referred to as the "Conditions for Processing" or "Legal Basis for Processing" or "Lawful Processing."

It is important that you determine your legal basis and document this in the registry of activities and/or in the DPIA (if required). Note that the legal basis for processing is required only for the Data Controllers, not for the Data Processors.

There are six kinds of legal basis to process personal data:
1. The consent of the Data Subject.
2. The performance of a contract.
3. The legitimate interest of the Data Controller.
4. The legal obligation.
5. The protection of vital interest.
6. The public interest.

The next few pages address the different legal bases for processing to help you choose the most appropriate for your activities.

The Consent of the Data Subject

Obtaining the consent of the Data Subjects is the most obvious, but it comes with consequences. The consent must be explicit and requires an action from the Data Subject. The individual should be fully informed about the usage of their personal data. If they remove their consent later, you should take appropriate measures.

There are important aspects relating to consent:

- **Request:** When you request the consent, you must include the identity of the Data Controller, the purposes of processing in clear and plain language for each activity (no bundled consent), and inform the individual of their right to withdrawal. The consent is never implicit or passive; there must be an action from the Data Subject. For example, this means that a sentence on a login page announcing that if the user logged in, s/he accepted the privacy terms is not active and is therefore not considered consent.

- **Withdraw:** The consent can be withdrawn at any time and easily (e.g. if the consent is given with one click, the withdrawal must be possible with one click). When the consent is withdrawn, note that the effect only applies to the future, not to the data collected when the consent was effective.

- **Keep evidence:** When you use consent as the legal basis for a processing activity, you should keep clear evidence about the authorization given by the individuals and the withdrawal.

- **Not linked with contract performance:** Contract performance must not be conditional on consent. This means that, according to

GDPR, the service that you offer must not be conditional on the consent given by the individual. To some extent, this means that the user should be able to use your service without giving you their consent.

- **Data portability:** By using the consent as the legal basis, you should offer data portability for the collected personal data (as discussed in more detail in the section on data portability).

In short, consent should be verifiable and individuals generally have more rights when you rely on consent to process their data.

The Performance of a Contract

In this case, you have a contract with the individual to provide a service or a product. In the scope of the execution of this contract, you need to collect personal data to provide the service. For example, if you provide insurance to cover a car, you need to identify the policyholder and the vehicle. The authorization to process the policyholder's personal data is based on the performance of the contract because you need the personal data to indemnify the policyholder.

The performance of a contract is an interesting approach because the Data Subjects can exercise their right of autonomy: they are always free to enter into the agreement (the contract).

Obviously, this legal basis by itself will rarely be enough since you cannot collect much information. GDPR introduces the concept of data minimization, which means that you have the right to collect and process only the personal data required for the execution of the contract. All other processing activities (e.g. direct marketing or big data analysis) should be legitimized through other legal bases (e.g. consent or legitimate interest).

The Legitimate Interest of the Data Controller

Rather than relying on a Data Subject's consent, the Data Controller may rely on its own legitimate interests, except when such interests are overridden by the interests or fundamental rights and freedoms of the Data Subject.

To meet the condition of "legitimate interest," the processing must be "necessary," meaning it should be the only existing way to achieve this legitimate interest. It cannot just be potentially interesting. The processing will not be considered "necessary" if there is another way of meeting the legitimate interest while also interfering less with people's privacy.

A Data Controller relying on this legal basis should inform Data Subjects about its legitimate interest. This legitimate interest must also be legally acceptable, and the interests of the Data Controller and the Data Subjects must be well balanced.

When carrying out the balancing test, three factors have to be considered:

1. the assessment of the controller's legitimate interest (commercial and/or societal benefits);

2. the impact on the Data Subjects (potential positive and negative impacts); and

3. the safeguards applied by the Data Controller to prevent any undue impact on the Data Subjects.

Attentive readers will notice that the balance test is similar to the DPIA and the logic behind it is similar even if a complete DPIA is not required.

The Legal Obligation

This legal basis covers the case of legal obligation, which is when the processing is necessary for compliance with a legal requirement. Examples of these cases include retention of accounting documents or disclosure to the courts.

The Protection of Vital Interest

If the processing activity is a necessity to protect the vital interests of a person, the processing of that personal data is authorized. For example, in a hospital, to save the life of an individual, personal data can be collected and processed, even sensitive health-related data.

Note that even though you are allowed to process the data without consent, you cannot ignore the regulations or safeguards for this information. Indeed, security and organizational measures are especially important in the case of healthcare data.

The Public Interest

In this case, the processing is necessary for the performance of a task carried out in the public interest or as an exercise in the capacity of an official authority vested in the Data Controller. To be recognized as a public interest, it must be written in national law.

What Legal Basis Can be Used for Some Real Cases?

This section reviews some real cases for using the legal basis for processing activities to be authorized.

Human Resources and Employee Data

To manage an organization, the employer processes employees' data. The following are just a few examples: to review employees' achievements; to keep track of employees' location outside of the office; Human Resources (HR) purposes including maintaining contracts, payment of salary and storing/using bank account details; or to protect economic/commercial/financial interests of the organization.

The use of consent as a legal basis can be considered inappropriate because of the subordinate position of the employee (is it really freely given consent?). In the HR case, you cannot rely on one legal basis to fulfil this criterion; it is best to find a mix of legal bases from the six options described in this chapter.

We suggest using the basis of carrying out contract duties for all activities related to payroll, for example processing of billable hours, salary, identity data and bank account details.

Moreover, the employer needs to process certain data to manage employees' performance. For these kinds of processing activities, we suggest using the legitimate interest as the legal basis. Indeed, management of employees' performance is needed to safeguard commercial and economic interests of the employer, as long as it is well-balanced and transparent with the employees.

There are also legal obligations for each time the employer is compelled by law to process employee data, and this will fall into the legal basis of legal obligations.

Consent can, however, be used for one-off, time-specific requests (e.g.

publication of employees' pictures taken during company events).

Big Data Analytics

Big data analytics is high-volume, high-velocity and high-variety information that demands cost-effective, innovative forms of information processing for enhanced insight and decision-making. From the point of view of the individual concerned, big data analytics is secondary processing.

Let's look at the use of social media analytics. Just because people have put data on social media without restricting access does not necessarily legitimize all further use of it. The fact that data can be viewed by all does not mean anyone is entitled to use it for any purpose or that the person who posted it has implicitly given consent for further use.

A Data Controller relying on consent as the legal basis shall be able to demonstrate, at any time, that consent was explicitly given. Relying on consent means that the Data Subject can withdraw their consent at any time and the Data Controller must then stop any data processing activity about this Data Subject.

As a result, use of consent as a legal basis for the processing of personal data for big data analytics purposes is questionable. The validity of such consent could be very easily challenged with the consequences that the processing itself would be regarded as illegal.

Consequently, we suggest using a different legal basis for this case: the legitimate interest of the Data Controller.

Data Portability

Data portability is a new right for the Data Subject in the scope of GDPR and is directly related to the right of access. To recap, data portability means that the information should be provided when the Data Subject asks for it and should be provided in a structured, commonly used and machine-readable format.

To clarify, you should be able to provide an easy-to-download file consolidating all the personal data of the requester. This file must be usable by the Data Subject to transmit his/her personal data to another company (e.g. competitor) or simply to keep for themself. The personal data included in the file is the personal data related to the Data Subject that they provided at any point to the Data Controller. Any derived data does not fall within the scope of this process, meaning it does not have to be included.

Data portability is a requirement for businesses only if the legal base for the processing of the data is the Data Subject's consent.

Transparency with the Data Subject

To be as transparent as possible with the Data Subjects, we found that keeping a special page (titled "privacy") on our website was the most elegant solution.

On this page, we provide guarantees about the processing activities in the form of icons with short and clear explanations.

The icons that we used come from the Noun Project, which aims to build a visual language that anyone can use and understand (https://thenounproject.com).

The icons that we selected are in the toolbox along with the other files. See below for the explanations we used:

- **Collection:** We do not collect more personal data than the absolute minimum required for the purpose of each process.

- **Storage:** We do not store more personal data than the absolute minimum required for the purpose of each process.

- **Usage:** We do not process personal data for other purposes than those defined when collecting.

- **Disclosure:** We do not disclose personal data to third parties.

- **Selling:** We do not sell or rent personal data.

- **Security:** All personal data is encrypted on our systems.

For each of the above aspects, we added a green check or a red cross to show clearly what we are doing with the personal data. In addition to the explanation, if applicable, we added a contact form at the bottom of the page, allowing the Data Subject to request access to their data in a structured way.

International Transfer

GDPR allows personal data to be transferred to another country or an international organization in certain conditions. These conditions are like the framework set in the previous directive: GDPR allows the data to be transferred to countries whose legal regime is deemed by the European Commission to provide an "adequate" level of personal data protection.

First, it is important to define what an international transfer is. A transfer happens when the personal data is transferred from one country to another through various mediums (e.g. internet, DVD, USB stick, printouts) or when remote access to the personal data is provided.

GDPR defines the basic transfer rule as below:
- The personal data is allowed to circulate freely inside the EU.
- Transfer outside the EU is forbidden.

In addition to this basic rule, transfer mechanisms are described in GDPR. International transfers come with a high level of complexity that requires the support of law specialists, so we do not cover those mechanisms in detail.

We strongly suggest keeping the personal data inside the EU. If it is necessary to transfer the data to the United States, the Privacy Shield Framework (https://www.privacyshield.gov) is a good start. If you work with other countries, we recommend getting help from someone specialized on this legal matter.

8 HOW TO USE THE TEMPLATES?

This chapter explains the different templates included in the toolbox included with this handbook. The files are ready to use and are set under the Creative Common CC BY 4.0 license (https://creativecommons.org/licenses/by/4.0/).

Based on this license, you are free to:

- **Share**: Copy and redistribute the material in any medium or format.

- **Adapt**: Remix, transform and build upon the material for any purpose, even commercially.

Under the following terms:

- **Attribution**: You must give appropriate credit (a link to the website https://www.gdpr-handbook.eu), provide a link to the license (https://creativecommons.org/licenses/by/4.0/), and indicate if changes were made. You may do so in any reasonable manner, but not in any way that suggests the licensor endorses you or your use.

- **No additional restrictions**: You may not apply legal terms or technological measures that legally restrict others from doing anything the license permits.

Feel free to send your suggestions via https://www.gdpr-handbook.eu/.

Templates Available in the Toolbox

- Registry of Data Processing Activities (Data Controller) (XLS)

- Registry of Data Processing Activities (Data Processor) (XLS)

- Data breach report (DOC)

- Data Protection Impact Assessment (DOC)

- Set of icons for transparency (PNG)

The following section gives further details relating to the two types of registry and the DPIA. It is hoped that the data breach report and the icons for transparency are self-explanatory.

The Registry of Data Processing Activities for Data Controllers

As mentioned previously, the registry contains all processing activities on personal data conducted by your company. For each activity, you should check, investigate and document the details, the legal basis and the consent.

For this purpose, a spreadsheet is enclosed in the toolbox. Its use is simple: you add one row per activity and fill in the columns with required information.

As a first step, we advise you to only list all the activities and, afterwards, to look at their details. During the filling-in process, you will probably have to split activities in multiple rows to define different rules, based on the sensitivity of personal data. Ask your employees for their input, and ask them to describe their usual activities. You will no doubt discover some you are not aware of. It is crucial to capture that information to better protect the data processed by your business.

The columns are described below. Feel free to adapt the spreadsheet to your organization's needs. The fields described hereafter are considered to be a minimum requirement.

<u>IT systems</u>

The first columns are used to structure the different sets of activities and processes that exist in your company. In the spreadsheet, we started with the department and the IT systems or software that use personal data. This makes collecting information easier, each department in the company knowing which software they use daily.

Feel free to change this grouping according to your organization, if appropriate. From experience, this top-down approach is quite efficient. For custom, in-house software, you should ask your developers to show you the structure of the database. For vendor-supplied software, you can usually see it directly in the user interfaces. If not, ask your vendors. All files used by employees to store information (e.g. Microsoft Excel, Microsoft Access, Mailchimp, accounting software), even if difficult to identify, should be captured in the registry.

Activity

The second part requires collecting information from the different IT systems or software. An identifier must be defined for each activity (e.g. A1 or C1.2). This way, you can easily attach documents or other information with this identifier as a reference.

Even if the processing is in the same system or for the same activity, it is good practice to record multiple rows in the registry, each row related to a personal data category (e.g. identification data or health data). This granularity is especially convenient if you process data of different sensitivity levels because it will allow you to set different policies (e.g. for retention, transfer or consent) based on the category. Remember that data could come from different sources and you should think broadly: data coming from customers, data about employees, or data collected on the website or on social media, to name but a few. You should refrain from using terminology that is too generic (e.g. "Employee data" or "Customer data") and be more specific depending on the circumstances, for example identification data, financial data, personal characteristics, physical characteristics, life habits and transaction history.

The column "purpose of processing" briefly explains why you are processing the data. Writing an extensive explanation is not required; you should avoid being too generic with terms like "improve user experience" or "IT security." Clearer terms might be "HR and payment management," "accounting," "shareholder management," "supplier screening" or "travel administration."

The column "category of data subjects" refers to the type of individuals you are processing the data for, for example current and former employees, job candidates, HR administration staff, customers or suppliers.

The column "category of recipients" refers to any individual, legal entity, public authority or agency to which the personal data is disclosed. The best approach is to list all categories of people who have access to the data and split the record for each of them if a different policy is required. Do not forget to flag any recipients outside the EU. Examples of recipients include officers/directors, HR manager, HR administration staff, IT administrators, application developers, external IT maintenance company and facility management staff.

Policy and security measures

If you make international transfers, it should be referenced in your registry and it is necessary to set up adequate safeguards. Please also note that the National Supervisory Authority should be informed in case of any transfers outside the EU.

Fill in this cell to refer to an external document if you make any international transfers. An example of what to write is: "Yes: adequate safeguards described in document X."

The column "retention policy" refers to when data "expires" in your company and will be erased. Whether short or long term, the retention policy must be appropriate. You must set up a time limit for the deletion of the data and explain the reasons why you have applied this limit, for example "seven years due to accounting/tax rules" or "ten years due to fraud detection systems."

The general description of technical and organizational security measures refers to all activities that your company puts in place to protect data from security breaches such as hacking, misuse or accidental deletion. It covers the pseudonymization and encryption of personal data; the ability to ensure confidentiality, integrity, availability and resilience of the systems; the backup policy; and the regular testing process of the security measures. Most of the time, these aspects are part of a whole security policy. Fill in the cell with specific measures for this category of personal data and refer to a general policy for your company's IT security.

Data collection

The columns for this section refer to the legal basis for data collection.

There are two important aspects: the legal basis on how you got the data and the information delivered to the Data Subject (the individuals).

The legal basis is basically the "authorization" to use personal data for this specific activity. There are six main kinds of "authorizations" to process personal data; see Chapter 7 for more detail but here are the basic themes:

1. The consent of the Data Subject.
2. The performance of a contract.
3. The legitimate interest of the Data Controller.
4. The legal obligation.
5. The protection of vital interest.
6. The public interest.

One of the key aspects in data collection is data minimization. It means that you should collect only the data required for the process. You cannot collect additional data even if it might be useful in the future.

The second part of the data collection column refers to information delivered to the Data Subjects. The individuals must be fully informed about the purpose of the process, and from the moment you get his/her consent, you cannot use the personal data for any other purpose. It is good practice to keep track of the information already delivered to the Data Subjects to obtain their consent before enforcement of GDPR. Your registry should mention when the information was given to the Data Subject. Remember that you must always be able to show evidence of this communication, so keep it in your systems.

Data storage

These columns refer to the location of your data storage (your servers or the third-party service that you are using), who is operating it and the legal basis. In most cases, the data stays in the EU on your own servers or those of a third-party provider. In this case, further legal basis is not required. You should check and validate the privacy clauses in the contract with your provider.

Data access

After data collection and data storage, we must define its access. The first part deals with the legal justification to transfer or use the data, for example your payroll officer needs access to the personal data of your employees to pay them. In that case, the legal justification is the execution of the contract with the employee. If you should transfer the data to an authority on a regular basis, the legal justification is the legal obligation.

After justifying the access, security aspects need to be covered. In other words, data access must be secured to ensure that only the intended recipients can access the data. It could be a simple mechanism like the authentication of the recipient, for example using passwords or an ID card.

Third-party processor

If you are using a third-party processor for the data, you should fill in those columns. The goal is to have a quick overview of your third-party providers, to check the location of the data storage and to set up a data processing agreement to ensure the protection of personal data.

Data Protection Impact Assessment

When processing sensitive data, you must conduct a DPIA (See "Dig Deeper for High-risk Activities" in Chapter 3 for more details). It should only be conducted by the Data Controller for high-risk activities or for the processing of sensitive personal data. Again, use your common sense: if you think that the activity could be perceived as high risk by the Data Subjects, do a DPIA and keep track of it in these columns.

Comments/Action points

While collating the activities, you will notice actions to be done and/or some comments to be added. You can use these columns to keep track of your thoughts and the actions to take.

The Registry of Data Processing Activities for Data Processors

This is similar to the details given for the registry for Data Controllers. The template spreadsheet is enclosed in the toolbox. It is divided into two sheets: the registry itself and the list of Data Controllers.

The fields described hereafter are considered the minimum requirement. Feel free to adapt the spreadsheet to your organization's needs.

Data Controllers sheet

Let's start with the first sheet: Data Controllers. This sheet should be filled in with one row per Data Controller. It is a kind of contact list to identify the different Data Controllers for whom you are processing personal data. The columns are described below.

Data Controllers

First, an identifier (e.g. customer ID or VAT number) as well as a category should be assigned to each Data Controller. For example, if you are providing software as a service for the insurance industry, you will no doubt need categories such as "insurer," "insurance broker," "body shop" and "assessor." These values will be used in the registry of activities.

For each Data Controller, you will add the contact details of the Data Protection Officer or the person responsible for data protection if no DPO has been assigned. This list has to be up to date so the right persons can be reached when required.

In addition, it is useful to reference the contract and indicate if it includes clauses that apply to data protection (or a data use agreement).

The last columns are used to keep track of comments and/or actions regarding each Data Controller. This list should be reviewed at least once a year, preferably every quarter.

Registry sheet

The second sheet is the registry itself. It is very much like the registry for the Data Controller described in the previous section. It covers only technical aspects of the processing because the legal basis for the processing and/or the collection fall under the Data Controller's remit. Again, you simply add one row per activity and fill in the columns with the required information.

As a first step, we advise you to only list all the activities and, afterwards, to look at the details. During the filling-in process, you will probably have to split activities in multiple rows to define different rules, based on the Data Controller's categories. The columns are described below.

IT systems

The first columns are used to structure the different sets of activities and processes that exist in your company. In the spreadsheet available in the toolbox, we started with the service provided to the customers and the IT systems or software that handle personal data. By structuring the approach by service and software, you can drill down from the service offered to your customers (the Data Controllers) to software and systems that are used to provide this service.

Feel free to change this grouping according to your organization, if appropriate. From experience, this top-down approach is quite efficient. For custom, in-house software, you should ask your developers to show you the structure of the database. For vendor-supplied software, you can usually see it directly in the user interfaces. If not, ask your vendors. All files used by employees to store information (e.g. Microsoft Excel, Microsoft Access, Mailchimp, accounting software), even if difficult to identify, should be captured in the registry.

Activity

The second part requires collecting information from the different IT systems or software. An identifier must be defined for each activity (e.g. A1 or C1.2). This way, you can easily attach documents or other information with this identifier as a reference.

Even if the processing is in the same system or for the same activity, it is good practice to record multiple rows in the registry, each row related to a personal data category (e.g. identification data or health data). This granularity is especially convenient if you process data of different sensitivity levels because it will allow you to set different policies (e.g. for retention, transfer or consent) based on the category. Remember that data could come from different sources and you should think broadly: data coming from customers, data about employees, or data collected on the website or on social media, to name but a few. You should refrain from using terminology that is too generic (e.g. "Employee data" or "Customer data") and be more specific depending on the circumstances, for example identification data, financial data, personal characteristics, physical characteristics, life habits and transaction history.

The column "purpose of processing" briefly explains why you are processing the data. Writing an extensive explanation is not required: you should avoid being too generic with terms like "improve user experience" or "IT security." Clearer terms might be "HR and payment management," "accounting," "shareholder management," "supplier screening" or "travel administration."

The column "category of data subjects" refers to the type of individuals you are processing the data for, for example current and former employees, job candidates, HR administration staff, customers or suppliers.

The column "category of recipients" refers to any individual, legal entity, public authority or agency to which the personal data is disclosed. The best approach is to list all categories of people who have access to the data and split the record for each of them if a different policy is required. Do not forget to flag any recipients outside the EU. Examples of recipients include officers/directors, HR manager, HR administration staff, IT administrators, application developers, external IT maintenance company and facility management staff.

Policy and security measures

In you make international transfers, it should be referenced in your registry and it is necessary to set up adequate safeguards. Please also note that the National Supervisory Authority should be informed in case of any transfers outside the EU.

Fill in this cell to refer to an external document if you make any international transfers. An example of what to write is: "Yes: adequate safeguards described in document X."

The column "retention policy" refers to when data "expires" in your company and will be erased. Whether short or long term, the retention policy must be appropriate. You must set up a time limit for the deletion of the data and explain the reasons why you have applied this limit, for example "seven years due to accounting/tax rules" or "ten years due to fraud detection systems."

The general description of technical and organizational security measures refers to all activities that your company puts in place to protect data from security breaches such as hacking, misuse or accidental deletion. It covers the pseudonymization and encryption of personal data; the ability to ensure confidentiality, integrity, availability and resilience of the systems; the backup policy; and the regular testing process of the security measures. Most of the time, these aspects are part of a whole security policy. Fill in the cell with specific measures for this category of personal data and refer to a general policy for your company's IT security.

Data storage

These columns refer to the location of your data storage (your servers or the third-party service that you are using), who is operating it and the legal basis. In most cases, the data stays in the EU on your own servers or those of a third-party provider. In this case, further legal basis is not required. You should check and validate the privacy clauses in the contract with your provider.

Data access

The Data Processor must also ensure proper access to data is available, mainly meaning the security related to access. In other words, data access must be secure to ensure that only the recipients can have access. It could simply be authentication of the recipient (e.g. using a password or ID card) but could be more detailed depending on your business.

Data Controllers

As you are a Data Processor, you do the processing activities for the Data Controller(s), or for a category of Data Controllers. This column is the link between the Data Controllers sheet and the Registry sheet.

Comments/Action points

While collating the activities, you will no doubt notice actions to be done and/or some comments to be added. You can use these columns to keep track of your thoughts and the actions to take.

Data Protection Impact Assessment

For high-risk activities or for the processing of sensitive personal data, you must conduct a DPIA. It is a document written by the Data Controller (data owner) that identifies and minimizes the privacy risks of new projects or new practices.

In this document, the risks must be analyzed from the Data Subject's point of view. It must describe the likelihood and severity of the risks.

The minimum requirement is described below:

1. Systematic description of the processing and its purposes including, where applicable, the legitimate interest pursued by the Data Controller.

2. Assessment of the necessity and proportionality of the processing.

3. Assessment of the risk to the rights and freedoms of Data Subjects, considering the expectation of the individuals and the evaluation of the risk based on likelihood and impact.

4. The measures in place to address the risks, including safeguards, security measures and mechanisms (for example pseudonymization, anonymization, encryption, local storage, access restriction and limited retention).

We suggest the following eight sections are used as a template structure when writing the DPIA:

1. Executive summary.
2. Project description.
3. Purpose of processing.
4. Data flows.
5. Identification and quantification of absolute risk.
6. Mitigation of risk.
7. Assessment of risk and proportionality.
8. Consultation with Data Subjects (optional).

The first section is the **executive summary**. It describes the key points of the DPIA and should include a short summary, the description of the project, the purposes of the processing, the risks identified, the measures to minimize the risks and the residual risks.

The second section is an introduction and **description of the project**. The purpose is to provide a full description and the context of all data processing related to your project (remember that the DPIA must be done before starting the activity).

The third section is the **purpose of processing**. It must describe each purpose of personal data processing and how the requirements to lawfully process personal data are met. It should cover the types of personal data processing and the categories of personal data used.

The fourth section is a long one and covers all **data flows**. You should describe all of them, in the form of diagrams and tables of personal data being processed from collection to deletion (or anonymization). You should mention and describe when the data is processed by a Data Processor and any other potential recipients of the data.

The fifth section covers the **identification and quantification of absolute risk**. The personal data being processed should be categorized based on the risk of damaging and harming the Data Subject in case of security breach, which is what your organization considers the absolute risk defined as the maximum potential exposure of the group to a specific risk. This means exposure before controls and mitigation. A workshop should be conducted by the senior manager/DPO to identify those risks and share understanding in the organization.

The sixth section deals with **risk mitigation**. It explains how to address the absolute risk, including safeguards, security measures and mechanisms, both technical and organizational. After applying these measures, a residual risk usually remains. This section should clearly indicate how the technical measures comply with the principles of GDPR and its key articles, for example Art. 25, GDPR, Data Protection by Design, and Default and Art. 32, GDPR, Security of Processing. It should ensure personal data protection and demonstrate compliance with GDPR, in accordance with the rights, freedoms and legitimate interests of Data Subjects and other individuals concerned.

The seventh section, the **assessment of residual risks and proportionality**, is the heart of the assessment. An overall assessment should describe whether the personal data processed and associated residual risks are acceptable. It should also describe the necessity and proportionality of the processing. It should specifically clarify whether or not too much personal data has been collected and retained according to the original purposes that were explained to the Data Subject. The criteria defining the acceptable level of risk should be described and aligned with corporate risk appetite (a matter for the board of directors). The suggestions for further mitigation of risk should be described in this section.

Finally, and optionally, you could add a section on **consultation with Data Subjects**. Indeed, the best way to evaluate the risk is to involve Data Subjects and document their views on the necessity and proportionality of personal data processing. It is optional but highly recommended.

9 SOURCES

Unless otherwise specified, the details provided in this handbook are taken from the official document for REGULATION (EU) 2016/679 OF THE EUROPEAN PARLIAMENT AND OF THE COUNCIL, available at http://ec.europa.eu/justice/data-protection/reform/files/regulation_oj_en.pdf (last accessed November 16, 2017).

Some of the definitions have been drawn from text on Wikipedia, searched for using the bold, underlined text (last accessed November 16, 2017).

Printed in Great Britain
by Amazon